ANIMALS
Don't Wear Pajamas

A Book About Sleeping

By Eve B. Feldman
Illustrated by Mary Beth Owens

Henry Holt and Company   New York

First edition
Published by Henry Holt and Company, Inc.,
115 West 18th Street, New York, New York 10011.
Published simultaneously in Canada by
Fitzhenry & Whiteside Ltd.,
195 Allstate Parkway, Markham, Ontario L3R 4T8.

Library of Congress Cataloging-in-Publication Data
Feldman, Eve.
    Animals don't wear pajamas / by Eve B. Feldman; illustrated by
Mary Beth Owens.
    Summary: Describes what sixteen different animals do at bedtime,
including the elephant, sea otter, and parrot fish.
    ISBN 0-8050-1710-0
    1. Sleep behavior in animals—Juvenile literature.   2. Animal
behavior—Juvenile literature.   [1. Animals—Sleep behavior.
2. Animals—Habits and behavior.]   I. Owens, Mary Beth, ill.
II. Title.
QL755.3.F46   1992
591.51—dc20   91-25192

Henry Holt books are available at special discounts
for bulk purchases for sales promotions, premiums,
fund-raising, or educational use. Special editions
or book excerpts can also be created to specification.

Printed in the United States of America
on acid-free paper.∞

10   9   8   7   6   5   4   3   2   1

For my mother, Shoshannah Sidorov, a strong and
vibrant woman, who shares my enthusiasm for books and napping
—E. B. F.

For Anna Rose, with love
—M. B. O.

Animals don't wear pajamas, and they don't have ticking clocks to tell them when it's time to go to sleep. But animals do know when it's time to rest.

When darkness falls, it's time for hummingbirds to sleep. They need lots of rest after a full day of darting forwards, backwards, and sideways. During the day these tiny birds flap their wings so fast that the wings seem to disappear. All night long they sit perfectly still in a deep sleep. They won't move again until sunrise.

At night elephants lie down on their sides and go to sleep. They often snore. But after only two or three hours, their big, bulging bodies are no longer comfortable on the ground. So they wake up and rock themselves back and forth until they are on their feet again. If they are still tired, the elephants will have to finish their sleep standing up.

Some animals stay awake all night and do all their resting by day. The octopus is an underwater daytime sleeper. When the sun's rays filter down to the ocean floor, the octopus snuggles into a cave. Sometimes, the octopus wedges a shell in front of the cave's opening as if it were closing a bedroom door.

Lions sleep both day and night. Male lions usually sleep alone, and they may sleep as much as twenty-two out of twenty-four hours! Female lions spend most of their time with cubs and other females. They sleep less because it is their responsibility to hunt for food and care for the cubs.

Animals don't wear pajamas, and they
don't have bunk beds. But animals
do find comfortable places to sleep.

Gorillas build themselves a new bed every single night.
They bend a few branches, pile on twigs and leaves,
quickly creating a comfortable place to rest
their tired torsos.

Puffins sleep in one kind of bed in summer and another kind of bed in winter. In the summer puffins sleep in underground burrows. In the winter these red-billed birds sleep floating on the water with their heads turned back and tucked into their feathers.

Weary warthogs go to bed backwards. A warthog will back into a cave, a hollow space under rocks, or a dug-out den in the ground. If any animal comes to disturb it, the intruder will be scared away by the sight of the warthog's big, sharp tusks.

In tropical rain forests, basilisk lizards rest on very thin branches that hang out over the water. That way, if a snake slithers too close, the branch will shake and the lizard will land in the water, safely out of the snake's reach.

Animals don't wear pajamas, and they don't have cozy quilts.
But animals do have ways to make themselves warm
and cozy when they sleep.

Sea otters sleep floating in the water after wrapping themselves in strands of seaweed. These seaweed ties keep the otters from drifting away with the sway of the sea.

When a snow leopard sleeps, it curls its tail up around its body and over its nose. The leopard's long, furry tail is just right for blocking out the frosty winds.

Tired Chinese golden monkeys huddle and cuddle for comfort. They gather together wrapping their arms around each other, and stay that way for a long sleepy-time hug.

Perhaps the strangest blanket of all is made by the parrot fish. This bubblelike covering oozes out of the fish's skin. Each night, it can take as long as half an hour for the fish to produce its blanket. And it will take the fish the same amount of time to get free of this slimy covering in the morning.

Animals don't wear pajamas, and they don't have bedtime storybooks to read to their children. But many animal parents have special things they do for their young when it's time to sleep.

A mother deer tucks her fawns in for the night. She gently nudges the babies into a woodsy hiding place. The fawns stay put until their mother sounds a special wake-up-for-breakfast call in the morning.

Jewel fish fathers and mothers work together to get their young, called fish fry, to sleep each night. The mother jewel fish moves to the resting spot. She stays there, waving her body and her fins as a signal for her fry to come in to sleep. Meanwhile, the father jewel fish scurries around searching for any fry who are trying to stay up past bedtime. Gently but firmly, the father scoops up any strays in his mouth. Then he swims back, and blows the little fish into their nest!

A dolphin mother keeps her new calf positioned in a special spot under her side fin. As the mother moves, she uses her fin to create a current in the water that keeps the calf moving right by her side, even when it is sleeping.

When a gray wolf is a new father,
he will curl up to sleep
outside his family's den. He
guards his newborn pups and
their mother who sleep inside.

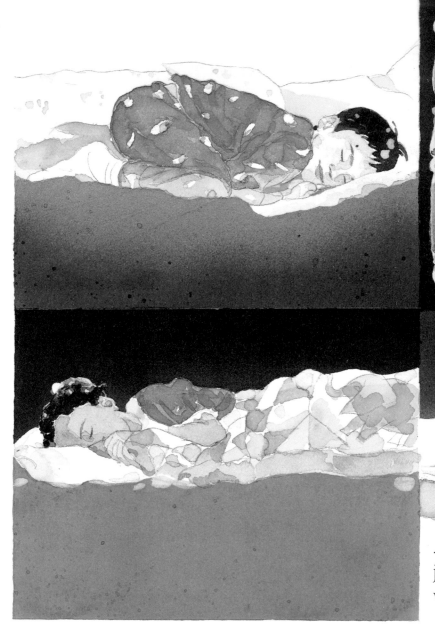

Animals don't wear pajamas. But animals, just like people, do have their own special ways to sleep.

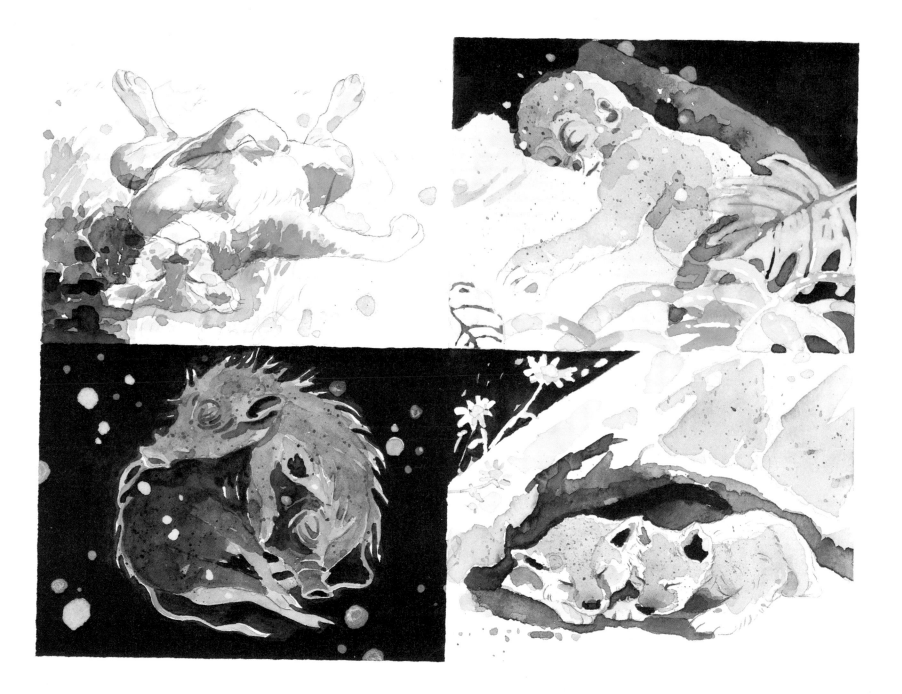

...When They Are Awake

Hummingbirds eat while flying. Their wings beat about sixty times a second, so fast that they make a humming sound—which explains how these tiny birds got their name.

Elephants spend their days chomping and chewing about four hundred pounds of roots, leaves, fruit, and grasses. All this eating wears down their teeth, but luckily the teeth grow back. This can happen as many as fourteen times during the life of an elephant.

Octopuses use their eight arms to propel themselves through the water. When they are awake and moving, octopuses swim backwards.

Lion mothers use other female members of their group, or pride, as baby-sitters when they leave their cubs to go off to hunt.

Gorillas wake up at sunrise and leave their nests to stretch. The leader of the group, a male with a silver-colored streak down his back, belches to give the signal for the others to follow him in search of plants for breakfast.

Puffin chicks are born in the summer. Puffin adults get ready for the birth by using their sharp beaks and webbed feet to dig out a nesting burrow. The puffin parents take turns sitting on their single egg. They also take turns feeding the chick after it has hatched.

Warthogs are not as fierce as they look. They'd rather flee than fight, and they can go as fast as thirty miles an hour.

Basilisk lizards can run a short distance on water without sinking. They can also stay underwater for quite a while if they have to.

Snow leopards prowl through the Himalayas, the highest mountains on earth. These cats' wide, hairy paws allow them to walk in the snow without getting cold feet.

Sea otters are very playful animals. They like to turn somersaults in the water and toss seaweed from paw to paw.

Chinese golden monkeys groom each other throughout the day, often making lip-smacking noises while they do so. Many of the other sounds they make come out of their upturned noses, instead of their mouths.

Parrot fish live in coral reefs where they use their strong, thick teeth to scrape off the algae from the rock-hard coral. Parrot fish got their name because some people thought that their mouths looked like parrots' beaks.

Deer can walk from the minute they are born. Mother deer hide their babies (usually twins) whenever they leave them. Even in zoos the mothers tuck the babies into hiding places. Often they hide the babies so well that the zookeepers can't find them!

Jewel fish swim in African rivers. The color of their skin changes with the seasons and with their moods.

Dolphins communicate with each other by squeaking, clicking, quacking, and whistling. They also make sounds that other dolphins can hear but people can't.

Gray wolf fathers won't enter their dens at all during the pups' first two weeks of life. When a new father returns from hunting with food to share with his mate, he drops it in front of the den.

Acknowledgments

The author wishes to thank the following people for sharing their expertise:

Carl Bennett, United States Department of Natural Resources
Bob Burhans, Scripps San Diego Aquarium
Helena Fitch-Snyder, San Diego Zoo
Mary Gunther and Jack Cover, Baltimore Aquarium
Dr. Steven Kress, The Fratecula Fund, Project Puffin,
National Audubon Society
Dr. Brenda Lavi, Nassau County Medical Center
Bob Porvine, University of Maryland, Department of Psychology
Joel Rubin, New England Aquarium
Paul Seiswerda, New York Aquarium
Dr. Barbara Smutz, University of Michigan, Department of Psychology
Roseanne Thiemann and Wendy Worth, Bronx Zoo